# F·E·A·R
## ADVENTURES

# FEAR
# AGENCY

## JAK SHADOW

Wizard Books

Published in the UK in 2006
by Wizard Books, an imprint of Icon Books Ltd.,
The Old Dairy, Brook Road, Thriplow,
Cambridge SG8 7RG
email: wizard@iconbooks.co.uk
www.iconbooks.co.uk/wizard

Sold in the UK, Europe, South Africa
and Asia by Faber and Faber Ltd.,
3 Queen Square, London WC1N 3AU
or their agents

Distributed in the UK, Europe, South Africa
and Asia by TBS Ltd., Frating Distribution Centre,
Colchester Road, Frating Green, Colchester CO7 7DW

Published in Australia in 2006
by Allen & Unwin Pty. Ltd.,
PO Box 8500, 83 Alexander Street,
Crows Nest, NSW 2065

Distributed in Canada by
Penguin Books Canada,
90 Eglinton Avenue East, Suite 700,
Toronto, Ontario M4P 2Y3

ISBN-10: 1-84046-726-6
ISBN-13: 978-1840467-26-0

Typesetting by Hands Fotoset

Printed and bound in the UK by Bookmarque Ltd

# Contents

# Introduction

Last summer you went to a holiday adventure camp. It was fantastic! Instead of teachers, real soldiers, explorers and athletes taught you how to do all kinds of things. You learned how to survive in dangerous lands, how to abseil down a mountain and how to crack secret codes. They even taught you how to track someone cross-country and how to avoid being followed.

On your last day at the adventure camp you were awarded five certificates and told that you were one of the best students they had ever had. You remember that final evening as if it were yesterday. Now, with your dangerous mission about to begin, you replay every detail of the scene in your head.

★ ★ ★

After a last campfire and a meal in the open air, one of the sergeants whispers in your ear.

'Colonel Strong would like to see you in his office. Please follow me. There is nothing to worry about; you haven't done anything wrong.'

You saw Colonel Strong on your first day. He is the officer in charge of the camp, a big man with a booming voice who is more than a little terrifying.

You cannot stop your knees from trembling, and your hands feel cold and clammy as you walk towards his office. You are wondering what on Earth he wants to talk about.

'My people have been watching you all week,' Colonel Strong begins. 'I know you have had a great time here and you've done extremely well. We are all very proud of what you have been able to achieve.

'It seems that you are exactly what we are looking for. Sit yourself down and let me explain,' he says, pointing to the chair.

'The world is in great danger. More danger than you could possibly imagine,' the colonel continues.

Why is the colonel talking to you like this? He obviously has more to say, so you wait for him to continue.

'My organisation is fighting a secret war against an evil alien genius.'

'But who is he and what does he want?' you ask.

'His name is Triton and he wants to rule the world,' the colonel tells you.

3

Colonel Strong passes you a photograph of Triton. He is like nothing you have ever seen before. He has green skin, piercing red eyes, pointed ears, a large nose and has strange lumps on his face. You would have no trouble in picking him out in a crowd.

'I have checked out your history and I have watched you all week. I know that you are loyal, honest and brave; but even so, I cannot tell you any more unless you swear a solemn oath to keep this secret.'

You are not too sure what the colonel means, but you know he is trustworthy and you long to hear more. You swear the solemn and binding oath that you will keep the secret.

'I work for an organisation called F.E.A.R.,' the colonel continues. 'It is an organisation so secret that only a handful of people in the whole world know about it.'

'But what is F.E.A.R.?' you ask.

'F.E.A.R. stands for Fighting Evil, Always Ready,' the colonel explains. 'I don't want you to feel you've been tricked, but this activity camp was specially set up to recruit the ideal agent,' he continues. 'We selected only children who we knew would be brave, strong, honest and, above all, quick-witted. We have watched you this week, and out of all the children, you are the one we have picked. We want you to become a F.E.A.R. agent.'

'Agent! What sort of agent? A secret agent?' you shout.

'Yes, a very secret agent. But I can only tell you more if you agree to join us. Or would you prefer it if we just forgot this conversation?'

'Of course I want to help, but I'm only a child. What could I possibly do?' you ask.

'All of our agents are children now. Triton has captured all our best adult agents, but he does not yet suspect our children.'

'Why can't we just hunt him down and kill him?' you reply.

'I wish it were that easy. The world Triton comes from is millions of miles from our planet, but somehow he has managed to get to Earth. He has a time machine and he is trying to change our time and our future. We have to stop him. We managed to capture one of his time machines, so now we've got one of our own.'

'You can count on me,' you say, smiling at the colonel.

'If you agree to become a F.E.A.R.

agent you will begin your training during
the school holidays. You have been
sworn to secrecy, and must not tell
anyone about the work you are doing.
We will tell your parents as much as they
need to know, but no more.'

Over the holidays since, your training is
nearly complete. You have worked hard
and learnt much. You know more about
Triton now, especially the fact that he
uses a time chip to take him back to a
particular time and place. If you can
take it from him, or destroy it, he will
have to leave. F.E.A.R. have made a
chip locator, and on every mission you
will take one with you. It will help you to
find Triton.

Now you are ready to begin your final
training mission, but Colonel Strong's

words are ringing in your ears:
'Remember you are facing a most
dangerous challenge and an evil enemy.
We have created a virtual reality Triton;
the image of him will react in exactly the
way the real Triton would. You will face
him four times in very different
situations.'

You wait for your instructions.

# How to Play

This is not like a normal book. Each section of the book is numbered. At the end of each section you will have a choice to make. Each of these choices will send you to a different section of the book. You make the choices and decide how you are going to deal with Triton.

If you fail, your mission will end and Triton will be able to continue his plan to take over the world. If you manage to combat all of the dangers Triton presents you will defeat him and be able to tackle the next stage of the mission. You must complete all four stages of the training mission to succeed.

# Your Mission

Colonel Strong is waiting for you at the F.E.A.R. base camp gate when you pull up in the army jeep, driven by his sergeant, Harris.

'Although this is a virtual reality mission, the dangers are still real,' begins Colonel Strong. 'Our computer boffins have worked hard on this program and it will not be easy.'

The colonel leads you into a room marked 'Mission Orientation Virtual Equipment'. In the centre of the room is something that looks suspiciously like a dentist's chair. You hope it won't be as terrifying!

'Right, you just sit here and put on the virtual reality helmet and think your way through the problems, nothing to worry about,' reassures the colonel.

'OK,' you reply, obeying the colonel and placing the helmet on your head.

Different coloured wires come out of the back of the helmet and snake off across the room, connected to computers with flashing lights.

'Comfortable?' asks the colonel, to which you simply nod. 'Four missions, you can do them in any order, just press the buttons marked 1, 2, 3 or 4. You can't move on to another mission until you have completed the one before,' he tells you, handing over a small keypad.

'VR computer engaged!' shouts a voice outside the room.

'Think the problems through and the computer does the rest,' says the colonel.

'Good luck,' he tells you, as he pats your shoulder, and then leaves the room.

'Just give me the thumbs up when you're ready,' says the other voice talking to you through a speaker on the wall.

You settle back in the chair, try to relax and close your eyes, hoping you are ready for what might face you.

Now read paragraph **1** to begin your adventure.

# The F.E.A.R. Agency

## 1

Slowly, you raise your right arm and give a clear thumbs up sign, then grit your teeth, ready for anything.

Suddenly the chamber feels as if it is spinning around and around. The room is swirling and fading, with different shapes appearing in front of your eyes. You hear a strange whooshing sound, like a strong wind. You keep spinning and then you feel yourself falling.

As the sound of the wind fades, a single shape appears before you. It is the keypad. It looks very strange, very 3D. Instead of the buttons being marked with numbers, there are slowly spinning objects.

The first looks like the Tower of London, the second an old-fashioned sailing ship, the third Big Ben and the last one a spaceship.

If you want to choose the Tower of London, turn to **44**. If you want to choose the sailing ship, go to **15**. If you decide to pick Big Ben, go to **27**. If you would rather choose the spaceship, go to **35**.

# 2

You head to the area behind the stage. There are lots of people around. Pinned on a wall is a list of all of the acts and the order in which they will play. The first person is the musician Gary Smile.

If you want to try to find Gary Smile, go to **11**. If you want to hunt for Triton, go to **3**.

# 3

You hunt around the whole of the backstage area, but find no sign of

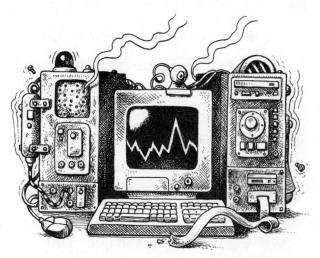

Triton. What is he up to, you wonder?
How could he use music to hypnotise
people? You realise that he must have
hooked something up to the sound
system. Sure enough, you find a
computer linked to the wires running to
the stage. The computer is on and ready.
Could this be it?

If you want to try to unplug the
computer, go to **12**. If you want to try
to find Triton instead, you should turn
to **33**.

# 4

The security guard grabs your hand and pushes it onto something that looks like a photocopying machine. Lights flash and you hear a whirring sound and the second security guard stares at his computer screen. He is reading the information.

'We've got no records of you. You don't exist!' he says, looking puzzled.

It is far too late and too complicated to try explaining now. The security guards will not let you go and you have failed your mission. If this was your first mission, go back to **1**. If you wish to try this one again, go to **35**.

# 5

The soldier leads you away from Traitors' Gate. You keep looking around to see if you can spot Triton. Then, at the

last minute, and too late, you spot him walking slowly towards the river, alongside a large man. He is going to escape! There is nothing you can do to stop him. You try to explain to the soldier, but he just ignores you and pushes you into the guardroom.

Perhaps it was not such a good idea to talk to the soldier? He would not understand your mission anyway. You have failed this time. If this was your first mission, go back to **1**. If you wish to try this mission again, go to **44**.

## 6

The storm is howling and rocking the ship backwards and forwards.

'We've sprung a leak, Captain. We're taking in water!' shouts one of the crew.

Just at that moment you hear a ripping sound. A huge hole has been torn in the side of the ship: she is sinking!

There is no way out of this. You have failed in your mission and the gold will be lost at the bottom of the sea. If this is your first mission, return to 1. If you want to try this one again you should go to 15.

## 7

You leap towards the three-headed alien. Whilst you are still in mid-air you feel an icy blast sweeping through you. You are frozen and cannot move! He must have been using an ice ray gun! Out of the corner of your eye you see Triton snatch up the smallest alien and pull off its head. Underneath is a different head, just like Felix's. So this must be the ambassador.

You cannot stop Triton from running off with him, protected by the three-headed alien.

You have failed your mission. If this was your first mission, go back to **1**. If you wish to try this one again, go to **35**.

# 8

You waste a second or two picking up the bag before you give chase. The rats are heading towards Docking Gate 574. It looks as if a flight has just arrived.

The rats pull a screen from the side of the wall and disappear up a tube. You are too late to stop them. But in front of you, three strange alien creatures have just come out of Gate 574. Behind, you can see Felix huffing and puffing, trying to catch you up.

Now turn to **37**.

# 9

'Oh, so you're a private detective then?' says the security guard.

You nod.

'He's not here yet and he won't come near here anyway,' he tells you.

'Right,' you say, 'thanks. Who's that screaming for help over there?'

The security guard looks through his top set of eyes.

'That's the ambassador's secretary,' he says, walking off.

If that is the ambassador's secretary, then you really ought to check him out and see what the matter is.

Now turn to **48**.

# 10

The creature is no more than ten metres from you, and manages to get in several shots before you reach him. All of them miss you. Just behind him you spot

Triton standing and smiling. Triton rushes past you and tries to get to the three aliens. You must act fast!

Do you want to try to stop Triton? If so, go to **58**. Or do you wish to deal with the three-headed alien and go to **7**?

# 11

A man with a clipboard walks past you. He seems to know what he is doing, so he might know where Gary Smile is.

'Do you know where Gary is? I've got something for him,' you tell the man.

'He's over there,' says the man, pointing but not even looking up at you.

You go over, but all you can see is an empty chair. Gary isn't there at all. Do you want to continue looking for Gary? If so, go to **24**. If you think it is better to try to find Triton, go to **3**.

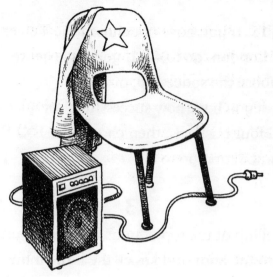

**12**

You yank out the leads to the computer and the screen goes blank. You hear Triton scream, but it is too late for him. His deadly plan has failed. You have beaten him!

The scene flickers in front of you, fades and then you see four 3D objects spinning in front of your eyes. If you have not yet chosen the sailing ship, go

to **15**. If you have not chosen the Tower
of London, go to **44**. If you have yet to
choose the spaceship, go to **35**.

If you have now successfully completed
all four missions, then choose the EXIT
symbol and go to **80**.

# 13

Yelling at the top of your voice, you jump
into the boat and knock the large man
into the water. He obviously can't swim
and is thrashing about wildly and
spluttering.

'Curse you! Take that!' screams Triton, swinging an oar at you.

Will you try to duck so that he misses you? If so, go to **61**. Or will you try to dive and grab Triton's legs? If so, go to **67**.

# 14

Even as you are carrying the sacks of gold ashore, you wonder if you can trust the villagers. There is no option. You need to stop Triton from stealing the gold. Each of the crew members has two sacks of gold slung over their shoulders and are struggling up the bumpy track towards the village.

You manage to get to the gate just in time, as Triton's ship docks alongside the jetty.

Luckily the village has a wall around it and some cannons, so you can defend yourselves. The village's leaders are not keen to fight pirates and want to give up and surrender you and the gold to Triton.

Will you let them do as they wish? If so, go to **74**. Or will you try to convince them that the village can hold the pirates off? If so, go to **68**.

# 15

'This is how Triton has disguised himself,' explains a clear, calm voice in your mind.

Before you is a photograph of Triton with a huge earring in his right ear. He has a spotted handkerchief around his

head and is wearing
a large hat with a feather stuck in it.
He looks like a pirate and you can even
see an old-fashioned ship behind him in
the photograph.

'Triton means to attack a treasure ship
and steal the gold. He will use this money
to cause more problems. Your mission is
to stop him. He may have henchmen
with him and will try his best to steal the
gold,' the voice tells you.

Suddenly you can feel wind rushing through your hair and the scene has changed completely. You are standing on the deck of a ship. The sails are billowing above you and the floor is gently rocking beneath your feet.

The deck of the ship seems deserted. Do you want to see if someone is steering the ship? If so, go to **70**. If you want to look below deck, in the cabins, you should go to **57**.

# 16

'You're carrying a lot of gold onboard, aren't you, Captain?' you begin.

She looks at you, wondering how to answer.

'And someone else knows you've got that gold. An evil pirate called Triton,' you continue.

'How do you know all of this? And what else do you know?' she asks, beginning to believe you.

Now turn to **36**.

# 17

You manage to squirm your way out from under the bed and slip through the crewman's grasping hands. He is big, but slow, and you run out of the door and up the steps onto the deck. You can hear him bellowing to the other crewmen to help him catch you. There is nowhere to hide, so you make for the edge of the deck and try to climb up the rope towards the sail. But you slip and find yourself falling overboard.

You have failed your mission. If this is your first mission, go back to **1**. If you wish to try this one again, turn to **15**.

# 18

You run along the gravel path towards Traitors' Gate. In olden times, this gate on the River Thames was used to bring in dangerous prisoners. As you reach the gate you can see that it is wooden and set into a huge stone wall. There is even a jetty for boats to be tied up to. You sense someone is there, and from the shadows you see a tall soldier marching along. He is obviously a guard. The man has a huge, fur hat and is armed with a rifle.

Do you want to hide and wait for the soldier to pass by? If so, go to **60**. Or do you think that it is a better idea to tell the soldier that Triton is trying to escape? If so, go to **40**.

# 19

You have saved the ambassador and completed your mission. Triton is struggling and staring at you with gritted teeth.

The scene flickers in front of you and fades. You see four 3D objects spinning in front of your eyes. If you have not yet chosen the sailing ship, go to **15**. If you have not chosen Big Ben then go to **27**. If you have yet to choose the Tower of London, turn to **44**. If you have now successfully completed all of the missions, choose the EXIT symbol and turn to **80**.

# 20

'I'm sorry Gary, I can't undo the knots,' you explain, standing up and then making for the stage area.

Even from the back, you cannot help but recognise Triton. He is dancing around and singing, pretending to be Gary Smile. The music is getting louder and louder. Then you notice a computer hooked up to the sound system. It has strange, wavy patterns on the screen and you know this must be part of Triton's plan.

If you want to try to unplug the computer, go to **26**. If you want to jump onto the stage and stop Triton from singing, go to **34**.

# 21

You try to run past the policeman, but he grabs you by the collar and hauls you back.

'Oi, you! No one gets in there without a pass. That's the orders,' he shouts.

He continues holding onto you and begins talking into his radio.

'Yep, I've got someone I want you to come and pick up,' he says.

In a couple of minutes a large, black van arrives and three policemen tumble out. The first policeman hands you over to them. There is no way you can stop Triton now.

You have failed in your mission. If this was your first mission you should return to **1**. If you want to try this one again, go to **27**.

# 22

You look around the floor, hoping to find a weapon, but all you can see is a small, wooden stool. At least you might be able to bash one of them with it. You crouch, picking up the stool, and with it in your hand you spring forward, yelling at the top of your voice. The large, bald man spins around and grabs the stool with one hand and your arm with the other. You can see Triton chuckling to himself, still inside the cell. But even as you struggle, he is squeezing through the gap in the bars and heading towards you with an evil grin on his face. Perhaps it was not such a good plan to try to tackle the pair of them on your own.

You have failed your mission. If this was your first mission, go back to **1**. If you wish to try this one again, go to **44**.

# 23

'What did this bloke that stole the backing music for your client look like then?' you ask the useless detective.

'Well, he was kind of green and warty. He must have some sort of skin problem,' the man replies.

There is no doubt that this is Triton and you need to find out as much information as you can.

'Who is your client and when is he or she playing?' you ask.

'It's Gary Smile and he is on in about an hour,' he tells you.

You are amazed that the man has given you this information, but at least you now suspect that Triton will use Gary Smile's music to hypnotise the city.

You thank the man and head off towards the stage, hoping that you might find Triton before he starts the music.

Now go to **72**.

## 24

You wonder where Gary might be. Then you hear a noise. It is a sort of grunting and groaning sound. You look behind a screen near the empty chair. A man in a suit has been tied to a chair and he has a rag stuffed into his mouth. This could be Gary. You pull the handkerchief out of his mouth and try to untie the rope.

'What is going on? Why has my music started?' the man asks.

Sure enough, the music has started. So this must be Gary Smile. Do you want to continue trying to untie him? If so, go to **52**. Or do you want to run towards the stage and try to stop the music? If so, go to **20**.

# 25

'OK, so you're watching something or someone, aren't you?' you say to the man, staring at his face.

Dark glasses hide his eyes and he looks rather embarrassed, as his cheeks have turned red.

'Am I that obvious?' he asks.

'Just a bit,' you say. 'So what are you doing here and who are you?'

'I'm working for one of my clients. He has had his background music tape stolen. I know what the bloke looks like. Funny looking man. I am hoping to catch him,' the man tells you.

If you think that what the man has told you is important and you need to know more, turn to **23**. If you think that this has nothing to do with Triton and his plan and want to go to the stage area, go to **72**.

# 26

You have no idea whether the computer has anything to do with Triton's plan, but you pull out the plugs anyway, just in case. As your hands grip the cables, you hear Triton scream 'No!' and realise that you have made the right decision. You have beaten him and his evil plan has failed.

The scene flickers in front of you and fades, and you see four 3D objects

spinning in front of your eyes. If you
have not yet chosen the sailing ship, go to
**15**. If you have not chosen the Tower of
London, go to **44**. If you have yet to
choose the spaceship, go to **35**.

If you have now successfully
completed all four missions, choose the
EXIT symbol and go to **80**.

# 27

'This is how Triton has disguised himself,
although he may have changed his

appearance
again by now,'
says a soft,
clear voice in
your head.

A photograph
of Triton in a
raincoat, with
the collar pulled

up around his face, appears in front of you. He has a black hat on his head, with a band of blue silk around it. He looks like some sort of spy.

'Triton wants to put London to sleep by hypnotising the people with music. Your mission is to stop him. He may have henchmen with him and he will try to make sure he succeeds,' the voice tells you.

Suddenly you can feel wind rushing through your hair and the scene has changed completely. You are standing on Westminster Bridge, staring at Big Ben and the Houses of Parliament.

It looks as if there is going to be a music concert in the square, as you can see a large stage and huge speakers. A band is practising on the stage. This must be how Triton aims to hypnotise Londoners.

There is an odd-looking man in a dark coat standing nearby, reading an upside-down newspaper. If you want to go and talk to him, turn to **76**. Or if you would prefer to check out the stage, go to **72**.

# 28

You roll yourself under the bed, hoping that whoever is coming into the room will not be able to find you. The parrot is leaping up and down, squawking and staring at you. Suddenly a large hand appears and tries to grab you.

If you want to try to get away, you should go to **17**. If you want to surrender, go to 77.

# 29

You flatten your body against the wall of the building, deep in shadows. Triton is walking alongside the big man and has his arm around his shoulder. They are laughing.

'I knew those muscles of yours would come in handy one day,' Triton tells the man.

'Yeah boss,' the man replies.

They don't seem frightened of being captured by any guards. They are walking along the gravel path towards the river. They must be heading for Traitors' Gate. They must be stopped!

If you wish to follow them along the path, go to **56**. If you wish to follow them but stay in the shadows, go to **63**.

# 30

The music begins to play, and the crowd gets ready for the first act. Many people are taking photographs of an empty stage and you wonder why. The music is getting louder and louder, and the crowd

is swaying, but not to the
music. You are beginning
to feel very sleepy. Too
late, you realise that
Triton is hypnotising the
crowd and the city with
the music.

You have failed your
mission. If this was your
first mission, return to **1**.
If you want to retry
this one, go to **27**.

# 31

'He's a very dangerous man! He's an
escaped prisoner and the other man
helped him get out of the cell,' you shout
to the Beefeater.

'That's impossible. No one can escape
from the Tower of London. Are you
trying to get me into trouble?' he replies.

'No, no, honestly,' you plead.

'All right then,' he says, still unsure that you are telling the truth.

He pulls a whistle out of his pocket and sounds three sharp blasts on it. In moments, soldiers, policemen and Beefeaters appear at every window and from every door.

'The youngster claims that a prisoner has escaped,' announces the Beefeater to the assembled crowd. Some are smiling, others are laughing. They don't believe you.

'I think we had better search everywhere, just in case,' says the Beefeater.

Unfortunately, in the confusion and delay, Triton has managed to get to Traitors' Gate and has disappeared down the River Thames in a rowing boat. Perhaps you should have dealt with Triton on your own?

You have failed your mission. If this was your first mission, go back to **1**. If you wish to try this one again, go to **44**.

## 32

'I think we should fight,' you say.

'All right,' says the captain. 'Load the cannons and wait for my order.'

In a few minutes Triton's ship is within range and the cannons fire, belching out black smoke. It does not stop Triton's ship and you can see him yelling instructions to his men on deck as they throw ropes towards your ship. They are going to try to clamber aboard.

If you want to stay and fight, turn to **66**.

If you think you should tell the captain to break away and run, turn to **39**.

# 33

As you continue to search for Triton, the backstage area is filling up with all of the acts that will play in the concert, making it even more difficult for you. Suddenly you see the unmistakable face of Triton. He is walking towards you. He is dressed up like a pop star. As soon as he sees you, he grabs a guitar and runs towards you, swinging it in his hands. You only have a second. Will you now try to unplug the computer? If so, go to **12**. Or will you rush to attack Triton? If so, go to **55**.

# 34

As you appear on the stage, you are grabbed by two of Triton's henchmen.

Triton turns around and gives you a wicked smile. Then he nods his head to his musicians, who turn up the volume. 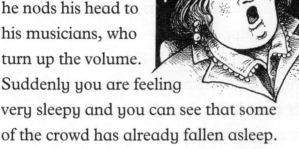 Suddenly you are feeling very sleepy and you can see that some of the crowd has already fallen asleep.

Triton has won and you have failed your mission. If this was your first mission, go back to **1**. If you want to try this one again, go to **27**.

### 35

This is how Triton has disguised himself,' a soft but reassuring voice announces in your head.

A photograph of Triton in a space helmet, with a microphone by his mouth, appears in front of you. He is wearing a spacesuit and seems to be in a spaceship.

'Triton is about to kidnap Ambassador Krun from the planet Halfor. If anything happens to the ambassador there could be war! Your mission is to stop him. He may have henchmen with him and he will stop at nothing,' the voice tells you.

'But what does the ambassador look like?' you ask.

Before you can get an answer you feel wind rushing through your hair and the scene has changed completely. You are inside a space station, packed with thousands of the weirdest aliens you could imagine.

'Help!' screams a voice.

The crowd begins to part, but you still cannot see who is shouting. If you want to see if you can help, go to **48**. If you want to ignore the cries for help, go to **78**.

# 36

'All I know is that Triton will try to attack your ship and steal the gold. That's why I'm here, to stop him,' you explain.

Even as you are speaking, one of the crew shouts out.

'There's a pirate ship in the distance. It's coming towards us!'

The captain raises her telescope to her eye and looks through it.

'We've got guns! We can protect ourselves!' shouts the captain.

'Since you're such an expert, what do you think? Should we fight him or run for it?'

If you think it would be better to fight Triton you should turn to **32**. If you think it would be safer to make a run for it, turn to **39**.

# 37

Felix is staring at the three strange aliens. He looks very confused. One of the aliens is a mix between a slug and a crab.

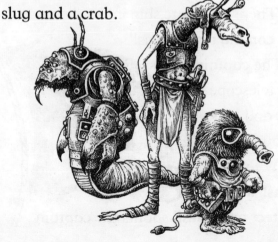

The second one is long and lanky, and has eyes on the end of stalks. The last one is tiny and has a hairy head, with a trunk like an elephant.

'OK, Felix, which one is the ambassador?' you ask.

'I don't know,' he answers.

'What do you mean, you don't know?' you say.

'He must be travelling in disguise,' Felix explains.

As you stand there, trying to work out which one could be the ambassador, you hear a gunshot from behind you. It narrowly misses the tallest of the aliens and they all duck down.

You turn to see a weird-looking creature, with three heads and six arms. He has a gun in each of his hands. Will you try to deal with the three-headed attacker? If so, go to **10**. Or do you think it is wiser to try to protect the three aliens? If so, you should go to **45**.

# 38

'They went that way!' shouts Felix, pointing towards the EXIT sign.

You run off in that direction, with Felix trailing behind you. As you reach the exit door you catch sight of the two rats. They spot you and dump the bag they have stolen from Felix.

If you want to chase the rats, go to **8**. If you want to pick up the bag and take it back to Felix, turn to **69**.

# 39

The ship manages to get away from Triton's pirate vessel. The wind picks up and blows the ship deep into the ocean. You can just see Triton's ship on the horizon, still trying to catch you. The weather is getting worse, and rain lashes the deck and the wind threatens to rip the sails.

'It's a tropical storm. Now we're for it,' says the captain.

She is unsure of what to do. She doesn't know whether to try to reach an island or stay out at sea in safety from Triton.

If you think the ship should try to find land, go to **64**. If you think it is safer to stay in the storm, go to **6**.

# 40

You step out of the shadows and immediately the soldier swings his gun around and threatens you with his bayonet.

''alt! Who goes there?' he shouts at the top of his voice.

'One of your prisoners is trying to escape,' you explain.

'Wot! 'ow did you get in 'ere?' he replies.

'I just told you!' you answer.

'You'd better come with me,' he says, poking the bayonet in your direction.

If you don't mind being taken prisoner by the soldier, go to **5**. If you think you should run for it, go to **53**.

# 41

You rather regret picking up a huge, black box containing a drum kit. But you manage to stagger towards the policeman. He just nods at you as you walk past him. You dump the box as soon as you dare and head for the stage. Four scruffy men are practising their act and no one seems to be watching or listening to them. There does not seem to be anything of interest and the loud noise is beginning to hurt your ears.

If you want to stay where you are, go to 75. If you want to look backstage, go to 2.

# 42

Try as he might, Triton cannot wriggle out of your hold. He is thrashing at you with his arms, but you just cling on. The pilot of the spaceship appears out of Gate 574 and stares for a second at the two of you struggling.

'Come and help me!' you shout.

The pilot drops his helmet and rushes over. He grabs Triton's arms.

'I've got him,' says the pilot.

You let Triton go and see that the attacking, three-headed alien has run off and left Triton. Felix is talking to the alien with the hairy head and trunk. As you join them he pulls off his disguise. You can see that this must be Ambassador Krun.

Now turn to **19**.

# 43

The little hairy-headed alien has only got tiny legs and you catch up with him, picking him up off the floor. He struggles for a second and in the struggle his head falls off!

Underneath you can now see that it is
Ambassador Krun. He looks exactly like
Felix. You place him back on the floor
and then worry about Triton. But he
cannot do anything. A pilot has arrived
and has grabbed him. The crab-slug
man and the other alien are also helping.

Now turn to **19**.

## 44

'This is how Triton has disguised
himself', a strange
but soothing voice
announces in your
mind.

A photograph
of Triton in an
overcoat, with a
scarf wrapped
around his neck
and a tall hat on

his head, appears in front of you. He is wearing a pair of glasses and is carrying a walking stick.

'Triton is about to escape from his prison cell in the Tower of London: your mission is to stop him. He may have henchmen with him and he will try to escape through Traitors' Gate,' the voice explains.

Suddenly you can feel wind rushing through your hair and the scene has changed completely. You are inside the Tower of London, standing on the grass. Just beside you is a sign saying 'Please Keep Off the Grass'. You step off it before you make your first decision.

If you want to go straight to the prison cell and try to stop Triton from getting out, you should go to **49**. If you want to lie in wait for him near Traitors' Gate, which leads to the river and freedom, go to **18**.

# 45

As you reach the three aliens, the crab-slug man grabs your arm with one of his pincers. You struggle to get free and, as you do so, you see Triton running towards you. He is protected by a ferocious six-armed, three-headed alien, who has a gun in each of his hands.

Triton is heading for the smallest alien. This must be the ambassador. The crab-slug man seems confused and lets you go. If you wish to stop Triton you should turn to **58**. If you want to try to deal with the three-headed alien, go to **7**.

# 46

For a second you stare at the wall and then see an enormous cog with a handle at the side of the jetty. This must close the gate, and you can reach it before they can stop you. Luckily it only takes five turns of the cog for the gate to creak shut.

Triton is stamping and yelling inside the rowing boat, which is rocking wildly. The large man has already fallen in the water and is trying to get to the jetty.

You feel a whoosh of wind just by your ear. You look up to see Triton swinging an oar at you. Even as you take all this in, he is swinging the oar again. If you wish to duck, turn to **61**. If you wish to dive forward and grab Triton's legs, go to **67**.

## 47

Felix is in such a state that you cannot get any sense out of him. Luckily there is a spaceport information officer nearby. In the crowd he looks like a naked man, but as you get closer you can see that his lower body is that of a horse.

'Do you know what ship Ambassador Krun is coming in on?' you ask.

'Let me see. It would be Flight XBL from Halfor, Gate 574,' he replies.

You thank him and quickly look up at the direction signs. Gate 574 is over to your right. You can see that Felix is

trying to follow you through the crowd.
As you reach the gate you can see three
very odd creatures coming out of the
door to Gate 574.

Now turn to **37**.

# 48

You push your way through the crowd.
In front of you is a small figure of an
alien that looks a bit like a frog, but has
hooves like a horse. He is still screaming

for help at the top of his voice. You walk up to him and ask him what the matter is.

'I'm Felix, Ambassador Krun's personal assistant. Someone has stolen his bag! They just disappeared into the crowd,' he cries.

This is a good lead. You have already found the ambassador's assistant.

'What do they look like? Who did it?' you ask.

'Well, they were all furry, a bit like large rats,' the frogman tells you.

Do you want to help Felix to find the rats and get the bag back? If so, go to **38**. If you think it is more important to try to find the ambassador, go to **47**.

# 49

It is dark, but there are gas lamps throwing some light through the gloom and fog. You wonder where Triton's cell

 might be. Then
you see a large
man running
towards one of
the towers. You
follow him and
step inside the
door he has left
open.

Sure enough, he is one of Triton's
henchmen and you can just see Triton
pacing up and down, watching the
man bend the bars of his prison cell.
In a moment he will be out! You must
act quickly! Do you want to try to
deal with the large man and Triton on
your own? If so, go to **22**. If you would
prefer to wait in the shadows and try
to get a better chance to stop them,
go to **29**.

# 50

You stare at the parrot for a second and it stares back.

'Pretty Polly's got the key. Pretty Polly's got the key,' it squawks.

Sure enough, there is a tiny key on a chain around its leg. You take it from the chain and look for a keyhole it might fit. On the opposite side of the room there is a long crack in the wood. This must be the door. The key slides into a tiny hole in the wall and clicks as you turn it. As soon as you have the door open, the parrot starts flapping and squawking. There is no other option but to hide! Someone will come!

Now turn to **28**.

# 51

The captain leaves a few of her crew onboard the ship to try to repair it as best they can. The rest of you begin walking towards the village. You are barely halfway there when Triton's ship arrives alongside the jetty. His men scramble onto the jetty and seize the captain's ship. There is no way you can get back to the ship in time to stop him. He will be gone before you can get there. Even from this distance you can see that Triton looks very pleased with himself.

You have failed your mission. If this is your first mission, return to **1**. If you would like to try this one again, go to **15**.

# 52

'Untie me! Untie me! Hurry up, untie me! This is my big chance. Millions of people will be watching this!' screams a desperate Gary.

You cannot seem to untie the knots and the music is getting louder and louder. You are beginning to feel very sleepy. You realise that Triton has succeeded and in minutes all of London will be asleep.

You have failed your mission. If this was your first mission, return to **1**. If you want to try this one again, go to **27**.

## 53

'Oi, stop!' shouts the soldier, as you spin around and run off into the darkness.

For a minute or so you can hear him huffing and puffing, muttering to himself. But soon you leave him behind. You are still looking back when you suddenly collide into something, or someone. You are knocked off your feet.

As you look up, you see a very strange-looking man, with an enormous collar, weird hat, and a waxed beard and moustache. This must be one of the Beefeaters. They live in the Tower of London and guard the crown jewels, which belong to the royal family of England.

'What are you doing here? Up to no good, I bet!' the Beefeater says to you, helping you to your feet.

'No, I'm not,' you begin to explain.

But just at that moment you see Triton and a large man walking along the path towards Traitors' Gate.

Now turn to **31**.

# 54

You decide not to tell the captain what you know. She looks very angry and shouts to one of her crew to lower a boat. A large crewman grabs you and drops you into the boat. He then cuts the rope that is holding it to the ship.

'If you won't help me, we'll be better off without you,' shouts down the captain.

You have been cast adrift and you have failed your mission. If this is your first mission, go back to **1**. If you want to try this one again, go to **15**.

# 55

You rush forward, narrowly missing Triton's swing with a guitar. It whistles past your head and you bundle into him, knocking him over.

'Get him! Hold him! We can't let him

stop us!' Triton shouts to two large henchmen.

The two men grab you and Triton stands up and brushes off the dust, smiling.

'Soon you'll all be asleep and I'll be able to do exactly what I want with London,' he says, turning and flicking on the computer.

The music begins to get louder by the second. You have failed in your mission and Triton has won. If this was your first mission, return to **1**. If you wish to try this one again, go to **27**.

# 56

Hard as you might try, your shoes make crunching noises on the gravel. You scrunch up your face, hoping that no one will hear you. But at that second Triton spins around.

'Get him!' he orders the large man. You must run, otherwise they will catch you. You are faster on your feet than the large man. But you suddenly collide into something, or someone. You are knocked off your feet. As you look up, you see a very strange-looking man, with an enormous collar, weird hat, and a waxed beard and moustache. This must be one of the Beefeaters. They live in the Tower of London and guard the crown jewels, which belong to the royal family of England.

'What are you doing here? And who are those two?' the Beefeater says to you, helping you to your feet, then pointing at Triton and the large man.

Now turn to **31**.

# 57

The steps creak as you slowly walk down the stairs into the gloom below. There is only one door to be seen. It, too, creaks loudly as you push it open. You look inside and realise that this must be the captain's cabin. There is a bed, wardrobe and table with charts all over it. In the corner there is a perch, and staring at you, with its head to one side, is a brightly coloured parrot.

If you want to walk over to the parrot and talk to it, go to **50**. If you want to look around the cabin, turn to **71**.

# 58

You grab hold of Triton around his waist as he tries to brush past you. It is a real struggle and he is stronger than he looks. The three-headed gunman is still firing at the three aliens. Suddenly the smallest of them runs. He must be the ambassador.

Do you want to continue struggling with Triton? If so, go to **42**. Or do you want to let go of him and try to protect the smallest alien? If so, go to **43**.

# 59

'So you're not talking? You look like trouble to me,' the security guard says to you. 'You'd better come with me. We'll check you out.'

It looks as if he is going to take you away and ruin your mission. Do you now want to tell him why you are here? If so, go to **9**. Or do you want to stay quiet? If so, go to **4**.

# 60

The soldier marches past without spotting you and disappears around the corner of a building. You crouch in the shadows, but can hear nothing except the lapping water around the stone wall. Nothing is happening and you wonder whether Triton is really trying to escape.

You wait for what seems like ages, but it is only a few minutes. Perhaps it was not a good idea to lie in wait for him. It may be better if you ran back to check the prison cell.

Now turn to **49**.

# 61

With all his might, Triton swings the oar at you. But he misses! He loses his balance in the rowing boat and tips into the water. As he comes up for air, his top hat floating away, he curses you.

You stand and smile as police, soldiers and Beefeaters arrive at Traitors' Gate. Two men wade into the water and clap Triton in irons before they drag him off. You have stopped him and completed this part of your mission.

The scene flickers in front of you, fades and you see four 3D objects spinning in front of your eyes. If you have not yet chosen the sailing ship, go to **15**. If you have not chosen Big Ben, go to **27**. If you have yet to choose the spaceship, go to **35**.

If you have now successfully completed all four missions, choose the EXIT symbol and go to **80**.

# 62

'So you want to stow away on my ship then? Don't think for one minute that I believe you. How did you get here, in the middle of the ocean? What are you really doing here?' demands the captain.

If you want to tell her the truth you should turn to **16**. If you think it is better not to say anything, go to **54**.

# 63

You follow them, dashing from one deep shadow to another. They have no idea they are being tracked. They finally reach Traitors' Gate and walk down some steps and out of sight. You speed up and run to the top of the steps. There is a rowing boat in the water at the bottom of the steps and they are both climbing into it. They must be stopped! You glance up and see that Traitors' Gate has been opened. They will be out and free on the River Thames in a minute or two.

Will you jump into the boat after them? If so, go to **13**. Or will you try to

close Traitors' Gate and stop them from
escaping? If so, go to **46**.

# 64

The crew manages to nurse the ship out
of the eye of the storm and into slightly
calmer waters. Triton is still in sight, but
some distance behind you.

'Land ahoy!' shouts one of the crew.

'Thank goodness for that,' says the
captain. 'Make for the harbour.'

In little more than half an hour you
reach a tiny island, with only a wooden
jetty in the harbour. The island is
definitely inhabited because there is a
track, and in the distance you can see a
village, with smoke rising from its
chimneys.

'So what do we do now?' says the
captain. 'You got us into this.'

You can either try to get help from the

villagers and leave the gold onboard,
or you can take the gold off the ship and
try to hide it in the village. If you want
to leave the gold, go to **51**. If you want to
take the gold, go to **14**.

# 65

'Aim the cannons at them! Fire at them
before they can attack!' you shout,
leaping up onto the top of the wall.

The five cannons fire and the
cannonballs fall amongst Triton's men,
sending them into confusion. Some of
them run off, but Triton just stands there,
staring at you and shaking his fist.

To your horror, two more pirate ships
appear on the horizon and a horrible,
smug smile spreads across Triton's face.
He knows that it is only a matter of time
before he will be able to attack and
overrun the village and take the gold.

You have failed your mission. If this was your first mission, return to **1**. If you want to try this mission again, go to **15**.

## 66

Triton's men begin boarding your ship. You are heavily outnumbered and the fight will be over quickly. Triton climbs aboard and spots you.

'So you thought you could stop my little scheme then,' he taunts.

You have failed in your mission and Triton has captured the gold. If this was your first mission, go to **1**. If you want to try this one again, go to **15**.

## 67

You lunge at his legs, but as you fall forward he catches you on your shoulder with the oar. The force of his blow sends you spinning into the water. The water is not very deep, but it is very muddy and you cannot seem to move your feet. You see Triton pull the large man back into the boat. He gives the man the oars and they begin to row away. As the scene begins to fade you can still hear Triton laughing at you.

You have failed your mission. If this was your first mission, go back to **1**. If you wish to try this mission again, go to **44**.

# 68

You have a little bit of time, and you manage to convince the villagers that they can hold off Triton and his pirates. Triton and his men are getting organised near the jetty, pulling cannons onto the island to fire at the village.

You are not sure how to stop him, but there are two choices. You can fire the villages' guns at his men and hope to scatter them. If you wish to do this, go to **65**. Or if you want to try to sink his ship with the cannons, go to **79**.

# 69

The rats disappear around the corner. You pick up the bag and run back to Felix. He is very grateful and relieved to have the bag back, but he is in a terrible state and panting for breath. You cannot get any sense out of him. There is obviously trouble here and you really need to find the ambassador.

Now turn to **47**.

# 70

You make your way to the back of the ship, seeing no one on your way. When you reach the deck you see the captain, standing with her back to you. She spins around, drawing her sword, and demands to know who you are and what you are doing on her ship. You wonder whether to tell her the truth.

If you want to tell her that you were lost at sea but managed to swim to her ship and climb aboard, turn to **62**. If you think she needs to know the truth and the reason why you are here, go to **16**.

# 71

There are clothes strewn all over the cabin, half-empty bottles of whisky and rum, scraps of food and no doubt plenty of rats. There is something not quite right

about the far wall. As you run your
hands around it you find a tiny crack all
around a section of the wood. This must
be a secret door. There is no handle, but
there is a tiny keyhole. There is probably
little hope of finding the key.

Do you want to continue looking
around the room? If so, go to **73**. Or do
you want to talk to the parrot? If so,
go to **50**.

Do you want to continue looking
around the room? If so, go to **73**. Or do
you want to talk to the parrot? If so,
go to **50**.

## 72

There is a high, metal
fence between you and
the stage. There is
one gate, which
is guarded by a
policeman who is
talking to a tourist.
You must get past
the policeman before

you can get to the stage. There is a pile of
musical equipment just beside you. You
could pick up one of the boxes and just
walk past the policeman. If you want to
try this, go to **41**. If you want to try to run
past the policeman while he is talking to
the tourist, go to **21**.

# 73

You do not manage to find anything of
use. All of a sudden you hear heavy
footsteps heading towards the cabin.
A large man wearing huge earrings

appears.
He has a red
scarf with white
dots tied
around his
head.
He is
wearing purple

trousers, a gold waistcoat and has a curved sword in his hand.

'A stowaway, eh? You'd better come with me to see the captain,' says the man.

He takes you onto the deck and marches you towards the back of the ship. When you reach the deck you see the captain, standing with her back to you. She spins around, drawing her sword, and demands to know who you are and what you are doing on her ship. You wonder whether to tell her the truth.

If you want to tell her that you were lost at sea but managed to swim to her ship and climb aboard, turn to **62**. If you think she needs to know the truth and the reason why you are here, go to **16**.

# 74

'We haven't got a chance against them,' says the mayor of the village.

'All right, tear off some white cloth from that sheet and wrap it around this stick. We'll surrender,' you say.

By now Triton and his men have reached the gate to the village. There are lots of them and they are heavily armed. Perhaps this was the right decision? You walk forward with your flag of surrender in your hand and Triton's men rush past you and grab the gold. At least the villagers will not be harmed, but you have failed in your mission. If this was your first mission, return to **1**. If you want to try this one again, turn to **15**.

# 75

Luckily, the awful band is finishing their practice session. You look around and see that the gates are being opened so the crowd can come into the concert arena.

There is no sign of Triton, or anyone that might look like one of his men.

Do you want to continue to wait in front of the stage? If so, go to **30**. Or do you want to look backstage? If so, go to **2**.

## 76

You walk up to the man, but he pretends not to notice you and continues reading his upside-down newspaper. You wonder whether you have done the right thing. He looks very odd and a shady character. He could be working for Triton. Are you sure you want to talk to him? If you do, go to **25**. If you have changed your mind and want to check out the stage, go to **72**.

# 77

'All right, I'll give up,' you say, crawling out from underneath the bed.

Above you is a large man with huge earrings. He has a red scarf with white dots tied around his head. He is wearing purple trousers, a gold waistcoat and has a curved sword in his hand.

'A stowaway, eh? You'd better come with me to see the captain,' says the man.

He takes you onto the deck and marches you towards the back of the ship. When you reach the deck you see the captain, standing with her back to you. She spins around, drawing her sword, and demands to know who you are and what you are doing on her ship. You wonder whether to tell her the truth.

If you want to tell her that you were lost at sea but managed to swim to her ship and climb aboard, turn to **62**. If you think she needs to know the truth and the reason why you are here, go to **16**.

# 78

You begin wandering aimlessly through the spaceport, pushing your way through the crowd. Already a huge, blobby alien has left slime all over your shoulder as he pushed past. You don't like the smell of it.

Perhaps if you got up higher and looked down you might see something useful? So you head for a staircase, but just as you get there a security guard grabs you by the arm.

'What you doin' 'ere?' he shouts at you.

Do you want to tell him you are here to protect the ambassador? If so, go to **9**. If you decide to say nothing, go to **59**.

# 79

'Fire at his ship! We need to sink it!' you scream, pointing at Triton's ship and urging the gun crews to get ready.

'No chance! That's too far away! We'll never hit it!' replies one of the gunners.

'We've got to try – it's our only chance,' you yell back.

The man does not seem convinced, but he orders the other gunners to get ready and they all fire at the same time. Four of

the shots land short and kick up sand and dirt, landing harmlessly. The fifth shot hits a rock and spins in the air. It hits Triton's ship just on the waterline.

In seconds Triton's ship begins to tilt over as it takes in water through the hole.

'We've done it!' you scream.

You look through your telescope and see Triton on his hands and knees, sobbing. He has been beaten and you have completed your mission!

The scene flickers in front of you, fades and you see four 3D objects spinning in front of your eyes. If you have not yet chosen the Tower of London, go to **44**. If you have not chosen Big Ben, go to **27**. If you have yet to choose the spaceship, go to **35**.

If you have now successfully completed all four missions, choose the EXIT symbol and go to **80**.

# 80

The scene disappears and you are back in the 'Mission Orientation Virtual Equipment' room. Colonel Strong walks in with a smile on his face.

'Well done! That's your last and hardest test. From now on you are fully operational. You are now an agent of F.E.A.R. I am sure you will be one of my best agents,' he says, shaking your hand.

You are very proud and pleased to have beaten the virtual Triton four times. You are also sure that you are now ready to face anything he might throw at you in a real mission.

Until then, you will have to wait. One day you will be called on for your first mission to save the Earth from this evil, alien genius.

Congratulations and welcome to the F.E.A.R. Agency!